THE RECIPES OF THE

Five Brothers

VOLUME III

Five Brothers One Passion

THE RECIPES OF THE FIVE BROTHERS ~ VOLUME III

Book Design: Bart Goodell
Photography: Jeff Weir
Writer/Editor: Leah Rosch
Recipe Development: Lynn Foley
                    Rosemary Smalberg
Food Styling: Michael DiBeneditto
Prop Styling: Sylvia Lachter
Hand Lettering: Bernard Maisner
Creative Direction: Jeff Brall
Digital Production: Rich Graham

Many thanks to all of these individuals who helped in making this book a reality; Julie Ying, Betsy Floyd, Lori Zoppel, Larry Kadish, Gail Young, Renée Tannenbaum and Jerry Simpson.

ISBN 0-9655889-2-0

Printed in China

A SANDY BOTTOM PRESS DESIGN

L'amore per la buona tavola
é amore per la vita

A passion for food is a passion for life

Contenuto

Introduzione

SUMMER TRANSLATES TO EASY COOKING AND ENTERTAINING NO MATTER WHICH SIDE OF THE ATLANTIC YOU'RE ON.

Fortunately, the many distinctive flavors of the season provide all the ingredients for creating tempting Tuscan dishes. Consider the wide array of vegetables, fruits, and herbs in season: eggplant, escarole, summer squash and fava beans, fresh tarragon and parsley, figs, peaches, plums, and sweet-tart berries. And then there are summer's crown jewels: vine-ripened, red tomatoes and fresh, aromatic basil—a combination that resonates CUCINA ITALIANA in its every regional variation. In Tuscan cuisine, these are the epicurean equivalents of an embarrassment of riches. These wonderful ingredients are used to prepare food that expresses the Five Brothers passion for eating well and living well, the same passion that inspired the exquisite sauces that bear the Five Brothers name and that you'll find at the heart of many of the recipes that follow.

But just because ease and simplicity reign doesn't mean summer food is unceremonial. The city of Siena, for instance, serves up exquisite fare of cured meats, fish, and herb-seasoned vegetable dishes to accompany the ceremonies of its centuries-old Palio festival, the famed horse races held every July 2nd and August 16th in the Piazza del Campo. And the summer solstice gets its due in starlit suppers shared on piazzas throughout the cities and towns of Tuscany.

Surrendering to the languid days and warm, breezy evenings, native Italians have managed to elevate the season's eating to an art form, simply by moving meals from indoors out.

These days, dining alfresco is as much a part of our summer vernacular as theirs. This is why you'll find three of the following four menus geared to the great outdoors; in the form of a shady meadow (or seaside) picnic and a savory backyard barbeque in which we celebrate the classic Tuscan-cooking characteristic of grilling practically everything in sight. The point to remember: savor the flavors of summer; they don't get much better than this.

Picnic per un bel giorno di sole

Picnic for a Perfectly Cloudless Day

This picnic offering is more like a moveable feast. The chilled soup will tastefully cool off a crowd. With a little advance prep, the three flavorful panini—sophisticated sandwiches with an Italian accent—can be ready to go in no time. And for dessert, a fresh, simple, delectable treat that tastes like summer. Load a cooler with ice, pack everything in and have a great time.

Zuppa di pomodoro fredda
chilled tomato soup

Pollo alla griglia con salsa d'olive su pane rustico
grilled chicken with olive pesto on peasant bread

Panini al gorgonzola con insalata di campo
wild greens and gorgonzola panini

Panini al tonno e ai carciofini marinati
tuna and marinated artichoke panini

Bruschetta dolce ai lamponi
dessert bruschetta with raspberries

wild greens and gorgonzola panini

Zuppa di Pomodoro Fredda

Chilled Tomato Soup

A refreshing summer soup (think gazpacho with Italian herbs) whose ingredients work well in several forms: diced, coarsely chopped or pureed.

3 CUPS TOMATO JUICE

2 CUPS FIVE BROTHERS™ FRESH TOMATO BASIL SAUCE

1 CUP PEELED, SEEDED AND CHOPPED CUCUMBER

½ CUP FINELY CHOPPED GREEN BELL PEPPER

¼ CUP THINLY SLICED GREEN ONIONS

3 TABLESPOONS TARRAGON VINEGAR OR CIDER VINEGAR

1 CLOVE GARLIC, FINELY CHOPPED

2 TABLESPOONS OLIVE OIL

2 TABLESPOONS FINELY CHOPPED FLAT-LEAF PARSLEY

1 TABLESPOON FINELY CHOPPED CHIVES (OPTIONAL)

½ TEASPOON FRESHLY GROUND BLACK PEPPER

In a large bowl, combine all ingredients. Cover and refrigerate at least 4 hours. Serve chilled. Serves 6.

chilled tomato soup

Pollo alla griglia con salsa d'olive su pane rustico

Grilled Chicken with Olive Pesto on Peasant Bread

Save time and cook the chicken breasts in advance. The zesty olive pesto that dresses these panini can liven up even leftovers.

- 2 CLOVES GARLIC, FINELY CHOPPED
- 3 TABLESPOONS EXTRA-VIRGIN OLIVE OIL
- 1 TABLESPOON BALSAMIC VINEGAR
- 2 BONELESS, SKINLESS CHICKEN BREAST HALVES (ABOUT ½ POUND)
- ¼ CUP CHOPPED FRESH FLAT-LEAF PARSLEY
- 2 TABLESPOONS CHOPPED PITTED GREEN OLIVES

- 1 TABLESPOON DRAINED CAPERS
- 1 TABLESPOON FINELY GRATED LEMON PEEL
- 1 TABLESPOON LEMON JUICE SALT AND COARSELY GROUND BLACK PEPPER TO TASTE
- 1 10-INCH FOCACCIA, ROUND SPLIT HORIZONTALLY

In a shallow bowl, combine 1 clove garlic, 1 tablespoon oil and vinegar. Add chicken; turn to coat. Cover and marinate in refrigerator up to 3 hours.

Meanwhile, for pesto, in blender or food processor, process parsley, olives, capers, remaining garlic, lemon peel, oil, lemon juice, salt and pepper until mixture has a coarse texture; chill until ready to serve.

Remove chicken from marinade, discarding marinade. Grill or broil, turning once, until chicken is no longer pink. To serve, slice chicken and arrange on ½ of the focaccia. Top with pesto, then cover with top focaccia. Cut into 6 wedges.

grilled chicken with olive pesto on peasant bread

Panini al Gorgonzola con insalata di campo

Wild Greens and Gorgonzola Panini

The pungent Gorgonzola has both a palatable and a practical use:
It's the tasty glue that holds these delicious sandwiches together.

8 OUNCES GORGONZOLA OR BLUE
CHEESE

1 10-INCH FOCACCIA, SPLIT
HORIZONTALLY

1 JAR (6 OZ.) ROASTED RED PEPPERS,
DRAINED AND SLICED

3 CUPS MIXED GREENS, SUCH AS
ARUGULA, ESCAROLE AND RADICCHIO

1 TABLESPOON EXTRA-VIRGIN OLIVE OIL

1 TABLESPOON BALSAMIC VINEGAR

SALT AND FRESHLY GROUND BLACK
PEPPER TO TASTE

Sprinkle cheese over bottom of split focaccia. Top with roasted red peppers, greens, oil and vinegar; sprinkle with salt and pepper. Cover with top of focaccia; cut into 6 wedges.

8

Panini al tonno e ai capriofini marinati

Tuna and Marinated Artichoke Panini

The rustic combination of tuna, artichokes, and black olive in these sandwiches is wonderfully evocative of Tuscan fare.

2 CRUSTY LARGE ROLLS, CUT IN HALF
HORIZONTALLY

2 TABLESPOONS BLACK OLIVE SPREAD

1 CAN (6½ OZ.) IMPORTED TUNA IN
OLIVE OIL, DRAINED

1 JAR (6 OZ.) MARINATED ARTICHOKE
HEARTS, DRAINED

½ CUP ARUGULA WATERCRESS OR TORN
LEAFY GREENS

Spread bottom halves of rolls with olive spread. Top with tuna, artichoke hearts and arugula. Cover with the tops of the rolls; cut each in half. Makes 4 half sandwiches.

Panini. AN APPRECIATION OF PANINI Literally speaking, PANINI means little breads. But what the word really refers to are delectable Italian-style sandwiches. And in a cuisine that respects bread as much as Tuscan, the pairing of a roll or two chunky slices of bread with a few fresh, flavorful ingredients is a natural. The breads that make the best PANINI: FILONE, cigar-shaped loaves; MICHETTE, which are round, hollow rolls; and thick slices of PANE TOSCANO, chewy rustic round loaves. But in a pinch, any crusty, quality bakery bread will do.

Bruschetta dolce ai lamponi

Dessert Bruschetta with Raspberries

*"Luscious" is the only word for this sweet treat. To transport,
pack all the fixings separately and assemble before serving.*

12 SLICES ITALIAN BREAD,
ABOUT ½-INCH THICK

⅔ CUP MASCARPONE OR CREAM
CHEESE, SOFTENED

2 TABLESPOONS HONEY OR
BROWN SUGAR

1 PINT FRESH RASPBERRIES

Lightly toast or grill bread slices. While still warm, spread with cheese. Drizzle with honey and
top with raspberries.

Serves 6.

Cenetta al Tramonto

Light Sunset Supper

This lovely meal works equally well indoors or out. In addition to its several choices and wonderful array of flavors, it's easy on the cook. Choosing between the two pasta selections will be difficult (they're both smashing). But each one is so simple that you practically can decide at the last minute which better suits the mood. To finish, a combo of the freshest fruit tastes of the season.

Crostini alle melanzane arrosto
crostini with savory roasted eggplant

Insalata fredda di radiatori
radiatore pasta salad

or

Farfalle con gamberi alla griglia
farfalle with herb-marinated grilled shrimp

Insalata verde con noci tostate e parmigiano
mixed greens with toasted walnuts and parmesan

Macedonia di frutta fresca
fresh fruit salad

farfalle with herb–marinated grilled shrimp

Crostini alle melanzane arrosto

Crostini with Savory Roasted Eggplant

A roasted red pepper is the secret ingredient here, infusing the eggplant mixture with a hint of rustic, smoky flavor.

1 SMALL EGGPLANT, PEELED AND SLICED

3 TABLESPOONS OLIVE OIL

½ CUP FIVE BROTHERS™ MARINARA WITH BURGUNDY WINE PASTA SAUCE

¼ CUP ROASTED RED PEPPERS, DRAINED AND CHOPPED

1 TEASPOON SMALL CAPERS, RINSED AND DRAINED

SALT AND FRESHLY GROUND BLACK PEPPER TO TASTE

1 CLOVE GARLIC

1 LONG LOAF (ABOUT 12″) ITALIAN OR FRENCH BREAD, CUT INTO ½-INCH SLICES (ABOUT 24)

2 TEASPOONS FRESH OREGANO, FINELY CHOPPED, OR ½ TEASPOON DRIED OREGANO

Preheat oven to 425° F. On lightly greased baking sheet, arrange eggplant; brush with 1 tablespoon oil. Bake 20 minutes, turning once; cool slightly. Decrease heat to 400°.

Coarsely chop eggplant, then combine with Five Brothers™ Marinara with Burgundy Wine Pasta Sauce, red peppers, capers, salt and pepper.

Using a fork to hold garlic, rub 1 side of bread slices with cut side of garlic. Brush both sides of bread slices with remaining oil, then sprinkle with oregano. On baking sheet, arrange bread slices and bake 5 minutes or until lightly golden. To serve, top with eggplant mixture.

Makes 24 crostini.

crostini with savory roasted eggplant

Insalata fredda di radiatori

RADIATORE PASTA SALAD

This is one of those perfect, all-purpose summer pasta recipes. Keep its uncomplicated ingredients on hand—you never know when you'll want to whip it up.

1 CUP FIVE BROTHERS™ FRESH
    TOMATO BASIL PASTA SAUCE
¼ CUP EXTRA-VIRGIN OLIVE OIL
3 TABLESPOONS BALSAMIC VINEGAR
1 TABLESPOON WHITE WINE VINEGAR
2 TABLESPOONS FINELY CHOPPED
    FRESH FLAT-LEAF ITALIAN PARSLEY
1 TABLESPOON FINELY CHOPPED
    FRESH BASIL LEAVES
½ TEASPOON SALT

¼ TEASPOON GROUND BLACK PEPPER
1 PACKAGE (14 OZ.) RADIATORE PASTA,
    COOKED AND DRAINED
3 MEDIUM RED, YELLOW OR GREEN
    BELL PEPPERS, CHOPPED
¼ CUP OIL-CURED OLIVES, PITTED AND
    SLICED
1 CUP DICED MOZZARELLA CHEESE
2 TABLESPOONS CAPERS, RINSED
    AND DRAINED

In small bowl, for dressing blend Five Brothers™ Fresh Tomato Basil Pasta Sauce, oil, vinegars, parsley, basil, salt, and pepper; set aside.

In a large bowl, combine pasta, bell peppers, olives, cheese and capers. Pour dressing over salad. Cover and chill until ready to serve.

Serves 6.

Farfalle con gamberi alla griglia

Farfalle with Herb-Marinated Grilled Shrimp

If you're in the mood for a little grilling, this
light, piquant pasta dish is a cinch—and pretty, too.

1 POUND EXTRA-LARGE FRESH SHRIMP,
   PEELED AND DEVEINED WITH TAILS ON
¼ CUP EXTRA-VIRGIN OLIVE OIL
2 TABLESPOONS BALSAMIC VINEGAR
1 TABLESPOON LEMON JUICE
1 TABLESPOON FINELY CHOPPED FRESH
   BASIL LEAVES
1 TABLESPOON FINELY CHOPPED FRESH
   FLAT-LEAF ITALIAN PARSLEY

1 TEASPOON FINELY CHOPPED FRESH
   OREGANO (OPTIONAL)
   PINCH CRUSHED RED PEPPER FLAKES
1 BOX (16 OZ.) FARFALLE OR PENNE
   PASTA, COOKED AND DRAINED
1 JAR (26 OZ.) FIVE BROTHERS™
   MARINARA WITH BURGUNDY WINE
   PASTA SAUCE

To butterfly raw shrimp, with small sharp knife, slice down back of shrimp, almost completely through. Spread and flatten to form butterfly shape. In shallow bowl, combine oil, vinegar, lemon juice, basil, parsley, oregano, and crushed red pepper flakes. Add shrimp, toss to coat. Cover and marinate in refrigerator 30 minutes.

Remove shrimp from marinade, discard marinade. Grill or broil shrimp, turning once, until shrimp turn pink.

Spoon Five Brothers™ Marinara with Burgundy Wine Pasta Sauce over hot pasta and top with shrimp. Garnish, if desired, with additional parsley.

Serves 6.

mixed greens with toasted walnuts and parmesan

Insalata verde con noci tostate e Parmigiano

Mixed Greens with Toasted Walnuts and Parmesan

*The walnuts and Parmesan add a welcome depth of flavor
and texture to this already charming salad of mixed exotic greens.*

8 CUPS MIXED SALAD GREENS
(ROMAINE, ARUGULA, ESCAROLE,
RADICCHIO, OR MESCLUN)

¼ CUP EXTRA-VIRGIN OLIVE OIL

2 TABLESPOONS BALSAMIC VINEGAR

SALT AND FRESHLY GROUND BLACK
PEPPER TO TASTE

¼ CUP COARSELY CHOPPED WALNUTS,
TOASTED

SHAVED PARMESAN CHEESE

In a large bowl, arrange greens; chill. In small bowl, combine oil, vinegar, salt and pepper. Pour dressing over chilled greens; toss to coat. Top with walnuts and shaved Parmesan.

Serves 4–6.

Macedonia di frutta fresca

Fresh Fruit Salad

The trick to this dish: combine as many varieties of fruit as possible. Allowing them to co-mingle in this citrus-juice marinade only enhances their fresh flavors.

2 POUNDS ASSORTED FRESH RIPE FRUIT
(SLICED PEACHES, MELONS,
NECTARINES, PLUMS, APPLES,
CHERRIES, FIGS AND BERRIES)

1 CUP ORANGE JUICE

¼ CUP SUGAR

2 TABLESPOONS ORANGE LIQUEUR
(OPTIONAL)

GRATED PEEL OF ½ LEMON

1 QUART VANILLA GELATO OR PREMIUM
ICE CREAM

In large bowl, combine all ingredients except gelato. Cover and refrigerate at least 4 hours. Serve with gelato.

Serves 6.

fresh fruit salad

Griglia del solstizio d'estate

SUMMER SOLSTICE BARBEQUE

Tuscans are grill crazy and once you taste these savory flavors, you'll understand why. Serve this menu to celebrate the summer solstice in June. Then bring it out again for your Labor Day FESTA. *It's fitting to bid farewell to summer in the same manner in which you ushered it in. Besides, for a real celebration, hot dogs and hamburgers can't hold a candle to this fare.*

GRIGLIATA DI MELANZANE, PEPERONI E ZUCCHINI
grilled eggplant, peppers and summer squash

POLLO ALLA GRIGLIA CON SALSA DI POMODORI ARROSTO
grilled chicken with roasted tomato sauce

— or —

TONNO MARINATO ALLA GRIGLIA
marinated grilled tuna

PENNE CON PISELLI E ZUCCA
penne with snap peas & squash

— or —

PANZANELLA
tuscan bread and tomato salad

PESCHE AL CHIANTI
peaches in chianti

Grilled chicken with roasted tomato sauce

Griglia di melanzane, peperoni e zucchini

Grilled Eggplant, Peppers and Summer Squash

For the most visually appealing presentation, select the freshest vegetables. To make a more substantial antipasto, serve with smoked mozzarella.

2 MEDIUM EGGPLANTS, PEELED AND CUT IN ¼-INCH SLICES

2 MEDIUM YELLOW SQUASH, CUT DIAGONALLY IN ½-INCH SLICES

2 MEDIUM RED BELL PEPPERS, QUARTERED

1 MEDIUM GREEN BELL PEPPER, QUARTERED

1 MEDIUM YELLOW BELL PEPPER, QUARTERED

⅓ CUP OLIVE OIL

½ TEASPOON SALT

½ TEASPOON GROUND BLACK PEPPER

2 CLOVES GARLIC, FINELY CHOPPED

In large bowl, toss vegetables with oil, salt, pepper and garlic. Grill or broil vegetables until tender, turning once. Arrange on serving platter and sprinkle, if desired, with chopped fresh basil leaves.

Serves 8-10.

Peperoni arrosto

ROASTING PEPPERS: *With a pair of metal tongs, hold the pepper over the flame of a gas stove or place it directly on the heating element of an electric stove. Turn, till each side is lightly charred and blistered. Then place the pepper in a closed paper bag to steam. When the pepper is cool to the touch, gently rub off skin by hand. Make sure to remove all traces of blackened skin—but don't rinse under running water, or you'll end up washing away the subtly smoky flavor as well.*

Pollo alla griglia con salsa di pomodori arrosto

GRILLED CHICKEN WITH ROASTED TOMATO SAUCE

*Charred tomatoes add a sweet–smoky flavor to the sauce—a
hearty–tasting accompaniment to the herb–marinated chicken.*

¼ CUP LEMON JUICE

¼ CUP OLIVE OIL

2 TABLESPOONS RED WINE VINEGAR

1 TABLESPOON FINELY CHOPPED FRESH
ROSEMARY (OPTIONAL)

2 CLOVES GARLIC, SLICED

¼ TEASPOON SALT

¼ TEASPOON GROUND BLACK PEPPER

8 BONELESS, SKINLESS CHICKEN
BREAST HALVES (ABOUT 2 POUNDS)

SALT AND FRESHLY GROUND BLACK
PEPPER TO TASTE

1 JAR (26 OZ.) FIVE BROTHERS™
OVEN ROASTED GARLIC &
ONION PASTA SAUCE

2 TEASPOONS GRATED LEMON PEEL
(OPTIONAL)

In large, shallow non-aluminum baking dish, combine lemon juice, oil, vinegar, rosemary, garlic, salt and pepper. Add chicken; turn to coat. Cover and marinate in refrigerator, turning occasionally, up to 3 hours.

Remove chicken from marinade, discarding marinade. Grill or broil chicken until no longer pink.

Meanwhile, in small saucepan, heat Five Brothers™ Oven Roasted Garlic & Onion Pasta Sauce with lemon peel. Serve chicken with heated sauce.

Serves 8.

Tonno marinato alla griglia

Marinated Grilled Tuna

This pesto marinade manages to improve on the already perfect taste of tender tuna steaks. To ensure not overpowering the fish, marinate for less than an hour.

1 CUP FRESH PESTO SAUCE* OR
  PREPARED PESTO SAUCE
½ CUP RED WINE VINEGAR

SALT AND FRESHLY GROUND BLACK
  PEPPER TO TASTE
2½ LBS. TUNA STEAKS, CUT 1-INCH THICK

In medium bowl, combine fresh pesto sauce, vinegar, salt, and pepper. Slice tuna into 10 servings (about 4 ounces each). Add tuna to pesto mixture; cover and marinate up to 1 hour.

Remove tuna from marinade, reserving marinade. Grill or broil tuna, turning and brushing with reserved marinade, until done.

Serves 10.

*FRESH PESTO SAUCE: In blender or food processor, process 2 cups fresh basil leaves, ⅓ cup extra-virgin olive oil, 3 tablespoons grated parmesan cheese, 2 tablespoons pine (pignoli) nuts, and 4 small cloves garlic until smooth.

marinated grilled tuna

Penne Con piselli e zucca

PENNE WITH SNAP PEAS AND SQUASH

*The combination of summer vegetables and this wonderful
grilled sauce gives this pasta dish the distinct flavor of summer.*

2 TABLESPOONS OLIVE OIL

1 LARGE CLOVE GARLIC, FINELY
   CHOPPED

2 CUPS SUGAR SNAP PEAS

2 MEDIUM ZUCCHINI AND/OR YELLOW
   SQUASH, HALVED AND SLICED

1 JAR (26 OZ.) FIVE BROTHERS™
   GRILLED SUMMER VEGETABLE
   PASTA SAUCE

1 BOX (16 OZ.) PENNE PASTA,
   COOKED AND DRAINED

In 12-inch skillet, heat oil over medium-high heat and cook garlic 30 seconds. Add vegetables and cook until crisp-tender, about 2 minutes. Stir in Five Brothers™ Grilled Summer Vegetable Pasta Sauce and heat through. To serve, spoon sauce mixture over hot pasta.

Serves 8.

Panzanella

Tuscan Bread and Tomato Salad

A delicious display of the reward of rejuvenating old and stale bread. Absorbing the vinegar's sharpness, the bread contrasts nicely with the vegetables' fresh flavors.

1 LOAF (¾ POUND) DAY OLD PEASANT
  BREAD (PREFERABLY WHOLE WHEAT),
  CUT INTO 1-INCH CUBES.

¼ CUP RED WINE VINEGAR

4 FRESH RIPE TOMATOES, COARSELY
  CHOPPED

2 SMALL RED ONIONS, QUARTERED AND
  THINLY SLICED

2 TABLESPOONS CHOPPED FRESH FLAT-
  LEAF PARSLEY

2 TABLESPOONS CHOPPED FRESH BASIL

½ CUP EXTRA-VIRGIN OLIVE OIL

½ TEASPOON SALT

¼ TEASPOON GROUND BLACK PEPPER

  ROMAINE LETTUCE LEAVES

In large bowl, sprinkle about ¼ cup water over bread, to moisten. Sprinkle with vinegar; toss lightly to coat. Stir in tomatoes, onions, parsley and basil.

In small bowl, blend oil, salt and pepper; toss with bread. Cover and chill at least 30 minutes.

To serve, line individual salad plates with lettuce leaves and top with salad.

Serves 8-10.

Pesche al Chianti

Peaches in Chianti

A beloved classic in Tuscany, probably because Chianti is the region's most renowned wine. For best results, use dark pink peaches and a lighter-bodied Chianti.

10 RIPE JUICY PEACHES
1 CUP CHIANTI WINE OR OTHER DRY WINE

In large stockpot, bring 3 quarts water to a boil. Add peaches, a few at a time, and boil 15 seconds. Immediately remove from boiling water and rinse with cold water until completely cool. Peel peaches, cut in half and remove pits. Slice peaches and place in shallow bowl, pour in wine. Cover and chill at least 2 hours.

To serve, arrange peaches in individual dessert bowls and garnish, if desired, with Amaretti biscotti or Anisette cookies.

Serves 10.

Cena al fresco

Outdoor Dinner Party

*N*o matter how casual the season's entertaining style, sometimes you want to make a splash. This menu does the trick with ease. The cioppino is a real show-stopper, the caponata is redolent of a Tuscan kitchen. And the tiramisù is one impressive dessert worth every last calorie.

Insalata di pomodori e mozzarella
tomato mozzarella salad

Cioppino alla toscana
tuscan fish stew

Caponata al forno
oven-roasted caponata

Tiramisù al lampone
tiramisù with raspberries

Insalata di pomodori e mozzarella

Tomato Mozzarella Salad

For unparalleled flavor, always pair the ripest tomatoes with the freshest mozzarella. Make it buffalo mozzarella (made from water-buffalo's milk) for melt-in-your-mouth creaminess.

6 RIPE TOMATOES, SLICED

8 OUNCES FRESH MOZZARELLA CHEESE, SLICED

FRESH ARUGULA OR LEAF LETTUCE

¼ CUP OLIVE OIL

2 TABLESPOONS BALSAMIC VINEGAR

¼ CUP FRESH BASIL LEAVES, SLICED (OPTIONAL)

On serving platter, alternately layer tomatoes and cheese over arugula. Drizzle with oil and vinegar and garnish with basil. Serve, if desired, with crusty Italian bread.

Serves 8.

Caponata al Forno

Oven-Roasted Caponata

This humble summer-vegetable medley has several tasteful applications: as a zesty side dish, buffet cocktail-party fare or even a light satisfying meal in its own.

1 LARGE EGGPLANT, PEELED AND
   DICED
1 MEDIUM RED BELL PEPPER, CHOPPED
1 SMALL ONION, CHOPPED
1 STALK CELERY, SLICED
¼ CUP FINELY CHOPPED OIL-CURED
   OLIVES
2 TABLESPOONS OLIVE OIL

1 TABLESPOON SMALL CAPERS, RINSED
   AND DRAINED
1 TABLESPOON RED WINE VINEGAR
2 CLOVES GARLIC, FINELY CHOPPED
   SALT AND PEPPER TO TASTE
1½ CUPS FIVE BROTHERS™ GRILLED
   SUMMER VEGETABLE PASTA SAUCE

Preheat oven to 425°.

In large roasting pan, combine all ingredients except pasta sauce. Stir in Five Brothers™ Grilled Summer Vegetable Pasta Sauce. Cover and bake 30 minutes.

Remove cover, stir, then bake an additional 30 minutes or until vegetables are tender. Serve at room temperature with toasted bread rounds, and garnish, if desired, with fresh parsley.

Serves 6.

Cippino alla toscana

TUSCAN FISH STEW

An Italian specialty retooled for regional distinction, this surprisingly
simple seafood stew is to be savored slowly for maximum appreciation.

2 TABLESPOONS OLIVE OIL

4 CLOVES GARLIC, FINELY CHOPPED

½ CUP VERMOUTH OR DRY WHITE WINE

18 LITTLENECK CLAMS, WELL SCRUBBED

1½ POUNDS MUSSELS, WELL SCRUBBED

1 JAR (26 OZ.) FIVE BROTHERS™
  FRESH TOMATO BASIL PASTA SAUCE

1 POUND FRESH OR FROZEN LARGE
  SHRIMP, PEELED AND SLICED

3 TABLESPOONS CHOPPED FRESH
  PARSLEY

2 TABLESPOONS CHOPPED FRESH BASIL
  LEAVES (OPTIONAL)
  FINELY GRATED PEEL OF 1 LEMON

In 8-quart stockpot, heat olive oil and cook garlic over medium heat 30 seconds. Add ¼ cup vermouth and clams. Cook covered over medium heat 8 minutes until clams open. Remove clams and set aside. (Discard unopened clams.) In same stockpot, add remaining ¼ cup vermouth and cook mussels, covered, 3 minutes or until mussels open. Remove mussels and set aside. (Discard unopened mussels.)

In same stockpot, add Five Brothers™ Fresh Tomato Basil Pasta Sauce, shrimp, parsley, basil and lemon peel. Return clams, mussels and any juices to stockpot. Simmer 2 minutes or until shrimp turn pink. Serve in shallow bowls and garnish, if desired, with toasted crusty Italian bread.

Serves 6.

Tiziana' al Carpone

Raspberry Tiramisù

The season's most sophisticated berries transform this classic dessert—a divine combination of Marsala, espresso and sweet mascarpone—into a brilliantly-hued, summertime taste treat.

6 LARGE EGG YOLKS

1 CUP SUGAR

1 CUP MARSALA WINE

½ CUP BREWED STRONG ESPRESSO
COFFEE, COOLED

1½ LBS. MASCARPONE CHEESE,
SOFTENED

1 PACKAGE (4 t - 6 OZ.) LADYFINGERS

12 OZ. FRESH RASPBERRIES

4 OZ. SEMI-SWEET CHOCOLATE,
FINELY CHOPPED

In top of large double-boiler, with wire whisk, beat egg yolks and sugar until light and fluffy, about 3 minutes. Whisk in ¾ cup Marsala wine. Place over boiling water. (Do not allow pan to touch boiling water.) Cook, whisking constantly, until egg mixture becomes creamy and doubles in volume, about 5 minutes. Remove from heat. Add espresso and cheese. Beat until smooth and creamy; set aside.

Brush both sides of ladyfingers with remaining ¼ cup Marsala wine. In large glass serving bowl or trifle bowl, arrange ¾ of the ladyfingers on bottom and sides. Pour half of the mascarpone mixture over ladyfingers. Top with ½ of the raspberries and chocolate. Repeat layers with remaining ladyfingers, mascarpone mixture, berries and chocolate. Chill at least 8 hours or overnight.

Serves 8.

*L'amore per la buona tavola
è amore per la vita*

A passion for food is a passion for life

Buon Appetito !

Share the Passion!
Join the Five Brothers Culinary Club

Send us your name and address on a 3½ x 5 card and you will periodically receive our free newsletter filled with inventive recipes and creative food ideas for unforgettable home meals.

Mail to: FIVE BROTHERS CULINARY CLUB
P.O. BOX 1210-B
GRAND RAPIDS, MN 55745-1210